Contents

Meat, Fish, Eggs, Beans, and Nuts

Meat and beans are foods that we eat.

Healthy Eating

Meat and Protein

Nancy Dickmann

Heinemann Library
Chicago, Illinois

www.heinemannraintree.com
Visit our website to find out
more information about
Heinemann-Raintree books.

To order:

 Phone 888-454-2279

Visit www.heinemannraintree.com
to browse our catalog and order online.

©2010 Heinemann Library
an imprint of Capstone Global Library, LLC
Chicago, Illinois

Edited by Siân Smith, Nancy Dickmann, and Rebecca Rissman
Designed by Joanna Hinton-Malivoire
Picture research by Elizabeth Alexander
Production by Victoria Fitzgerald
Originated by Capstone Global Library Ltd
Printed and bound in China by South China Printing Company Ltd

ISBN 978-1-4329-3981-6
14 13 12 11 10
10 9 8 7 6 5 4 3 2 1

Library of Congress Cataloging-in-Publication Data

Dickmann, Nancy.
  Meat and protein / Nancy Dickmann.
     p. cm. -- (Healthy eating)
  Includes bibliographical references and index.
  ISBN 978-1-4329-3981-6 (hc) -- ISBN 978-1-4329-3988-5 (pb) 1. Meat--
Juvenile literature. 2. Proteins in human nutrition--Juvenile literature. I. Title.
  QP144.M43D53 2011
  613.2'82--dc22
                               2009045482

Acknowledgements
We would like to thank the following for permission to reproduce
photographs: © Capstone Publishers pp.**5**, **12**, **14**, **22** (Karon Dubke);
Corbis p.**13** (© Image Source); Getty Images pp.**4** (Kevin Summers/
Photographer's Choice), **10** (Inga Spence/Visuals Unlimited), **11** (Dorling
Kindersley), **21** (Jon Feingersh/Iconica); iStockphoto pp.**8** (© Ronald
Fernandez), **23 top** (© Mark Hatfield); Photolibrary pp.**7** (Jo Whitworth/
Garden Picture Library), **9** (Animals Animals/Robert Maier), **20** (Peter
Mason/Cultura); Shutterstock pp.**6** (© BESTWEB), **15**, **23 middle** (© Juriah
Mosin), **16** (© a9photo), **17**, **23 bottom** (© Joe Gough), **18** (© Monkey
Business Images); USDA Center for Nutrition Policy and Promotion p.**19**.

Front cover photograph of meat, fish, eggs, nuts, and beans reproduced
with permission of © Capstone Publishers (Karon Dubke). Back cover
photograph reproduced with permission of iStockphoto (© Ronald
Fernandez).

We would like to thank Dr Sarah Schenker for her invaluable help in the
preparation of this book.

Every effort has been made to contact copyright holders of material
reproduced in this book. Any omissions will be rectified in subsequent
printings if notice is given to the publishers.

We also eat fish, eggs, and nuts.

Meat comes from animals such as cows.

Beans come from plants.

tuna

Fish comes from animals such as tuna.

Eggs come from birds such
as chickens.

Nuts grow on trees.

Eating these foods can keep us healthy.

Helping Your Body

Meat, fish, eggs, beans, and nuts all have protein.

You need protein to grow.

Eating beans gives you energy.

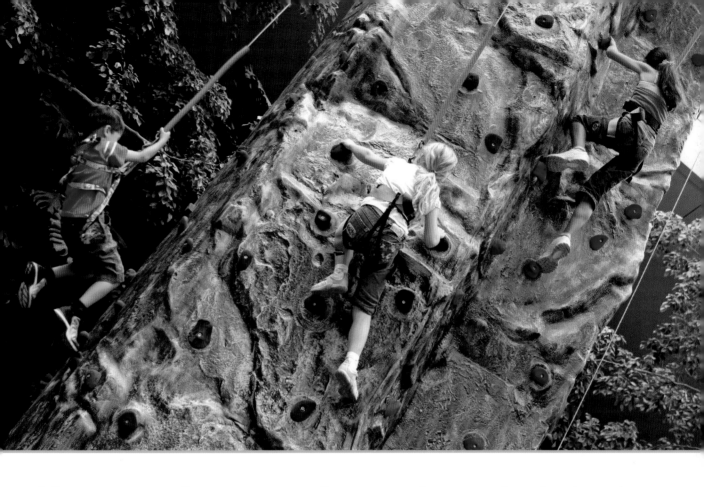

You need energy to work and play.

fish

Eating meat and fish helps keep your blood healthy.

Some meat has a lot of fat. Too much fat can hurt your body.

Healthy Eating

We need to eat different kinds of food each day.

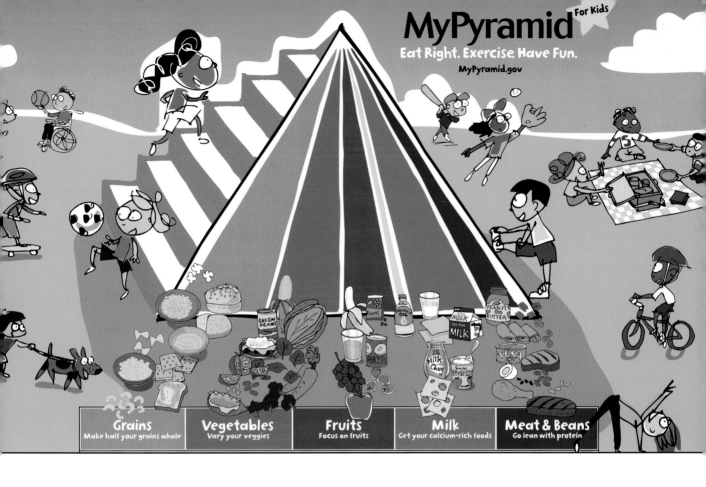

The food pyramid tells us to eat foods from each food group.

We eat meat and other protein foods
to stay healthy.

We eat these foods because they taste good!

Find the Meat

Here is a healthy dinner. Can you find a food made from meat?

Answer on page 24

Picture Glossary

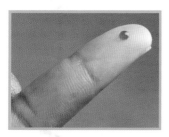

blood red liquid inside your body. Blood takes food and air to all your body parts.

energy the power to do something. We need energy when we work or play.

fat oily thing in some foods. Your body uses fat to keep warm. Eating too much fat is bad for your body.

Index

Answer to quiz on page 22: The meat food is chicken.

Notes for parents and teachers

Before reading

Explain that we need to eat a range of different foods to stay healthy. Introduce the meat and beans food group. Our bodies use protein from meat and beans to help build many of our body parts including our skin, hair, muscles, bones, and blood. Protein helps our bodies grow.

After reading

- Discuss the fact that some people do not eat meat and fish (vegetarians) and some do not eat meat, fish, eggs, or dairy (vegans). Brainstorm other foods they can eat to make sure they get enough protein.
- Explain that some people do not eat certain types of meat, or only eat meat that has been prepared in a certain way because of their religious beliefs. Buddhist: no meat or fish; Hindu: no beef; Jewish: Kosher meat, no pork or shellfish; Muslim: Halal meat, no pork; Sikh: no pork or beef. Share experiences of this as a class.